CLOUDS, RAIN, WIND, AND SNOW

BY MARTI ABBOTT AND BETTY JANE POLK

FEARON TEACHER AIDS

Torrance, California

Editor: Carol Williams
Copyeditor: Cynthia Seagren
Illustration: Tom McFarland
Design: Diann Abbott

ISBN 0-8224-1351-5

Printed in the United States of America
1. 9 8 7 6 5 4

Contents

Introduction

All too often teachers read a book to children to entertain them or fill some spare moments, and that is the end of it. With the closing of the book, teachers shut out children's responses and ideas. Teachable moments are lost forever. The Books and Beyond series provides teachers with creative activities and critical-thinking stimulators to maximize the effectiveness of good literature. A piece of literature can become the basis for a learning unit that spans many areas of the curriculum.

Each lesson in the Books and Beyond series begins with a brief synopsis of the book and introductory ideas to stimulate student interest. After reading the book aloud, the use of the critical-thinking and discussion questions will help children draw from their own related experiences and analyze, evaluate, and apply the message of the book. Follow-up activities that center around many curriculum areas and include a variety of teaching styles will help children move beyond the book and internalize its message.

Clouds, Rain, Wind, and Snow is a collection of lessons based on children's books that deal with various forms of weather. The lessons are a mixture of fact and fantasy. Children will gain scientific knowledge about the causes and effects of weather through experimentation and discussion. They will also enjoy the fun of creating art projects, writing stories, composing original poems, and using logical reasoning. Students will discover how we use the weather and its effects as a source of energy to make our work easier and as a source of fun to make our playtimes more exciting. The lessons also incorporate a variety of activities that will stimulate your students to think about how the weather affects the lifestyles of people and animals and how it affects our emotions and behavior.

Gilberto and the Wind

Written by Marie Hall Ets
New York: Viking Press, 1963

Synopsis

Gilberto has an unpredictable friend—Wind. Gilberto tries to play games with Wind. Sometimes Wind is helpful and other times it scares him. The two of them share whispers, roars, and finally stillness.

Introduction

Display the title page in *Gilberto and the Wind* showing Gilberto holding a kite. Have the children look at the expression on Gilberto's face and then speculate how Gilberto may be feeling and why. Ask the children to listen carefully as the story is read aloud to find out what Gilberto likes about the wind and what he doesn't like.

Critical-Thinking and Discussion Questions

1. Gilberto did not like Wind when it carried his balloon to the treetop, broke his umbrella, and would not help him fly his kite. What are some things you don't like about the wind?
2. Gilberto thought Wind was great when it would blow apples down from the tree for him, sail his boat, and blow his pinwheel. What are some things you like about the wind?
3. Gilberto was afraid of Wind when it started breaking trees and knocking down fences. Have you ever been afraid of the wind? When?
4. Have you ever tried to play with the wind? What did you do? Imagine what it would feel like. What kinds of things would be very difficult to do in the wind? What kinds of things could not be done without the wind?
5. Wind showed strength and power when it broke trees and knocked down fences. Wind could also be very quiet and still. Do you more often show strength and power or are you more often quiet and still? How do you act and what kinds of things do you do when you are showing strength or quietness?

Creative Writing Starters

Language Arts

The wind blew so hard one day that _____ .
I especially like to _____ in the wind because _____ .
I am afraid when the wind _____ .

Story Titles
The Giant Gust
The Kite That Wouldn't Come Down
My Wind-Powered Wagon

Personification

Language Arts

Gilberto personified the wind by giving it human traits and emotions. Gilberto says that Wind laughs, whispers, tries to take his umbrella away, squeezes through the door keyhole, and runs over the top of the grass. Give each child a sheet of lined paper. Encourage students to choose an element of the weather and write a paragraph that personifies their subject. Students might choose to write about rain, snow, hail, or fog.

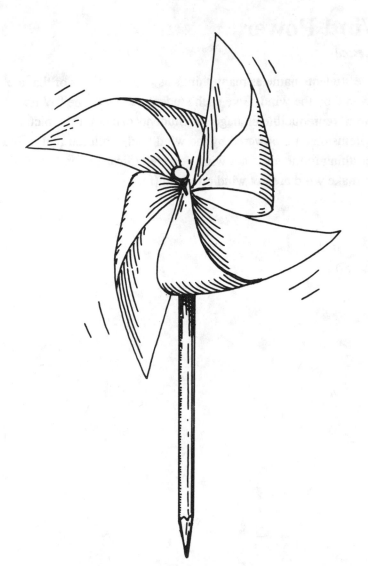

Whirling Pinwheels

Art

Give each student a copy of the "Pinwheel" reproducible on page
13. Children use crayons or markers to decorate both sides and then
cut the pinwheels out on the solid lines. Have children carefully cut
on each dotted line to make four slits in the pinwheel square. Have
each child bend the corner of the first section up so that dot 1 is over
the center of the square and then stick a pin through the backside of
the dot. Have children continue to bring each dotted corner to the
center and stick the pin through the backside of the corner. When all
corners are attached to the pin, stick the pin through the center of
the pinwheel and then into an eraser on the end of a new pencil. Be
careful not to crease the paper. Children can take the pinwheels
outside and play with the wind!

Wind Power

Science

Have students name as many things as they can think of that are powered by the wind. Give each student a copy of the "Wind Power" reproducible on page 14. Students can color the pictures of the items that are powered by the wind. Help children realize that everything in the air is not wind powered (airplane) and some things that make wind are not wind powered (fan).

Pinwheel

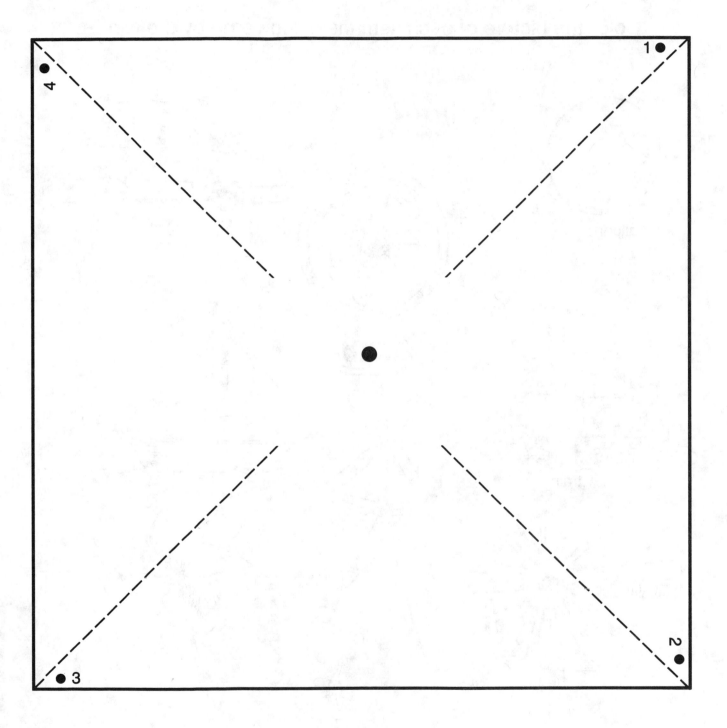

Clouds, Rain, Wind, and Snow © 1991 Fearon Teacher Aids

Wind Power

Color the picture of each item that is powered by the wind.

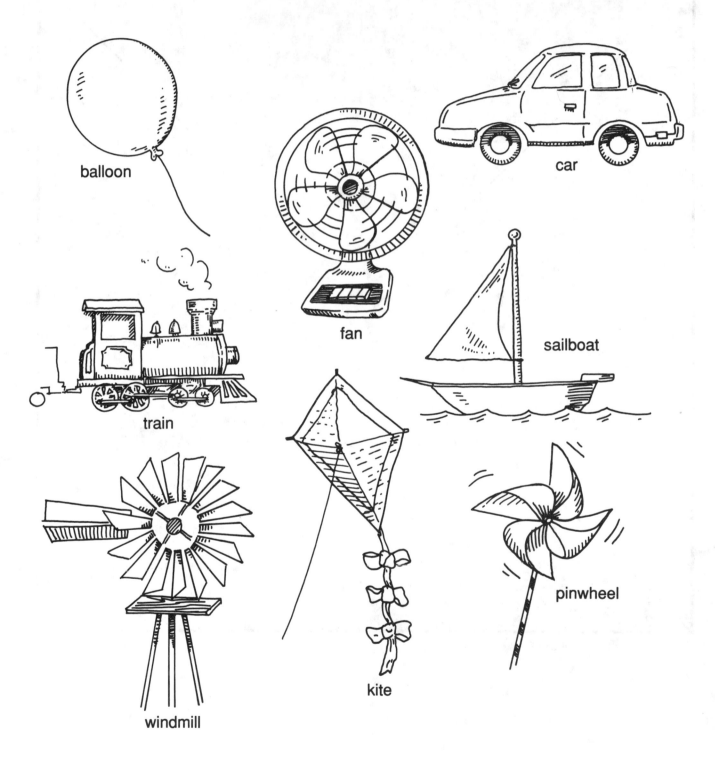

balloon

fan

car

train

sailboat

windmill

kite

pinwheel

Clouds, Rain, Wind, and Snow © 1991 Fearon Teacher Aids

Gilberto and the Wind

The North Wind and the Sun

A fable written by La Fontaine and illustrated by Brian Wildsmith
New York: Franklin Watts, 1964

Synopsis

The strong North Wind challenges the Sun to a contest. The Sun triumphs with his warmth and gentleness. The fable illustrates how gentle persuasion often succeeds when force fails.

Introduction

Ask children to describe the wind and the sun. Encourage children to think about ways the sun and the wind are alike and ways they are different. This story is about a contest between the wind and the sun. Invite children to listen closely as the story is read aloud to find out who wins the contest.

Critical-Thinking and Discussion Questions

1. The North Wind and the Sun had a contest to see who could make the horseman take off his cloak. The Wind lost the contest. Have you ever lost a contest? How did you feel?
2. Why do you think the North Wind chose to try to blow the cloak off the horseman's back as the contest? Do you think he chose that because he thought he would win? Have you ever been really confident that you could do something and then you were unable to? How did you feel?
3. At the end of the story, we are told that the Sun was warm and gentle and was able to accomplish more than the Wind with all his strength and fury. Do you think that gentleness can accomplish more than strength? Why or why not?
4. Are you more often gentle like the Sun or strong like the Wind? Which would you rather be? Why?
5. Do you think the contest was a fair one? Why or why not? Can you think of another contest the Wind and Sun could have? Who do you think would win that contest?

Creative Writing Starters
Language Arts

The wind is so strong that it can _____ .
The sun can get so hot that _____.
_____ is gentle and _____ is strong.

Story Titles
The Crazy Contest
The Day I Lost
Everyone Is a Winner

Wind and Sun Action
Language Arts

Discuss some of the effects of the strong North Wind and the warm Sun that were mentioned in the story. Give each child a copy of the "Wind and Sun Action" reproducible on page 19. Have children cut the verb cards apart and glue the verbs next to the appropriate nouns to describe the action in the story.

Strong or Gentle
Language Arts

Discuss the moral of the fable with the children. Help children see how the moral applies to their lives. Present familiar scenarios and encourage children to role play and react as the story characters did. For example, give one child a ball to play with. Ask another child to get the ball from the child as the Wind might have, using strength and force. Ask another child to get the ball by being as gentle as the Sun would have been. Continue with other role-play situations, allowing as many children to participate as possible. Follow up by discussing how children felt when they were forced to do something as opposed to being treated gently.

Wind Designs
Art

Ask children to recall some of the effects the Wind had in the story. Though most of them were negative, explain some ways that the wind can be helpful. Give each child a 9" x 12" sheet of black construction paper and a straw. Drop a few drops of diluted white paint in the center of each child's paper. Encourage children to aim the straw at the paint and blow into it to create an interesting wind-blown design. It is important that the straw does not touch the paint. For variety, try using bright colors of paint on white construction paper.

Heat and Color
Science

Ask children if they remember what color the horseman's cloak was. Look at the pictures in the book to verify their guesses. Ask children whether or not they think the color of clothing has any effect on how hot the clothing would be to wear. Try the following experiment to test their predictions. Put two identical thermometers outside in the sun. Cover one with black paper and one with white paper. Give each child a copy of the "Heat and Color Chart" reproducible on page 20. Children record the temperature on each thermometer in the correct column on their charts. Record the thermometer readings at 10-minute intervals for one hour. Encourage children to draw conclusions based on the results and to record the conclusions on their charts.

Wind and Sun Action

Cut off the bottom of the worksheet. Cut the action words apart. Glue each action word next to the correct noun to tell about the effects of the Wind and the Sun in the story.

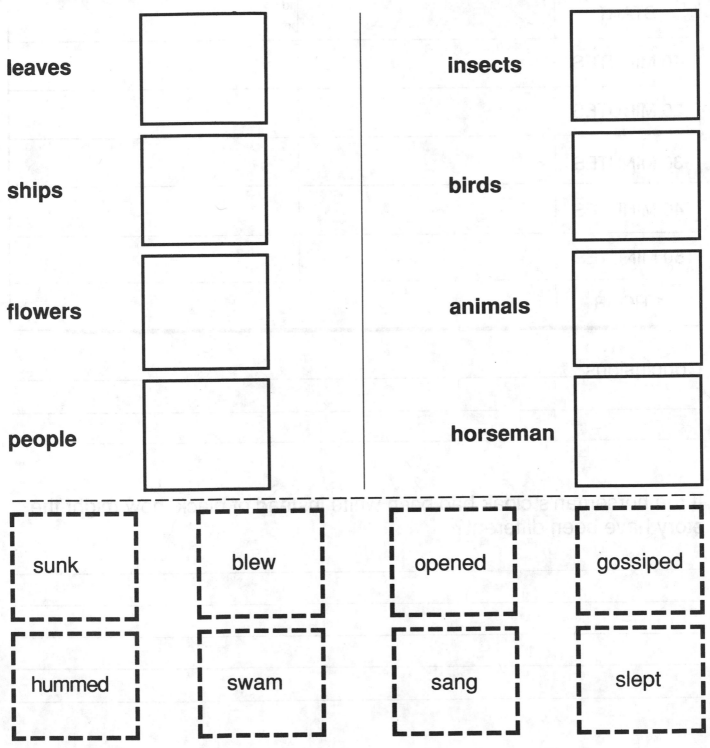

leaves

ships

flowers

people

insects

birds

animals

horseman

sunk

blew

opened

gossiped

hummed

swam

sang

slept

Heat and Color Chart

TIME	THERMOMETER UNDER WHITE PAPER	THERMOMETER UNDER BLACK PAPER
START		
10 MINUTES		
20 MINUTES		
30 MINUTES		
40 MINUTES		
50 MINUTES		
1 HOUR		

Conclusions: _____

_____

_____

If the horseman's cloak had been white instead of black, how might the story have been different?

_____

_____

_____

_____

The North Wind and the Sun

Clouds, Rain, Wind, and Snow © 1991 Fearon Teacher Aids

The Wind Thief

Written by Judi Barrett and illustrated by Diane Dawson
New York: Atheneum, 1977

Synopsis

The mighty wind decides he needs a cozy hat to keep himself warm. He notices a little boy wearing a striped stocking hat that looks just perfect. With one huge gust, he tries to blow the hat off the little boy's head. However, that one gust brings the wind more than he planned. The air is soon filled with every kind of hat imaginable, from baseball caps to Indian turbans.

Introduction

If possible, turn on a fan and aim it at the children so that they can feel the breeze as it passes by. Show children the title of the book and ask them what kinds of things they think the wind could "steal." Ask children if the wind has ever "stolen" something from them. Encourage children to listen closely as the story is read aloud to find out what the wind "steals."

Critical-Thinking and Discussion Questions

1. Why do you think the story is called *The Wind Thief?* What is a thief? Do you think the wind was a thief? Why?
2. Do you think the wind could really blow a hat off someone's head? What are some other things the wind could blow into the air? What are some things the wind could *not* blow into the air?
3. When the wind held his breath so that the hats would begin to fall back to the ground, they landed on the wrong heads. There were lots of funny mistakes. What kind of hat do you think would be a funny mistake on you? What kind of hat would you choose to wear?
4. The boy who lost his hat had tears in his eyes. How would you have felt if you had been that boy? Can you think of a clever plan the boy could have used for retrieving the hat? What?
5. Do you think the wind was wrong to take the boy's hat? Why or why not?
6. The wind felt bad about taking the little boy's hat when he saw how sad the little boy was. He thought about returning the hat to the boy. Why did the wind decide *not* to return the hat? Do you think he would have returned the hat if the boy had not gotten another one?

Creative Writing Starters
Language Arts

One day the wind blew my _____ and I _____ .
When the wind blows, I can _____ .
My favorite hat is a _____ .

Story Titles
The Funny Mistake
Dozens of Derbies
The Whistling Wind

The Big Wind
Language Arts

In the story, the effects of the big gust of wind were quite comical. People were walking at a slant, dogs were blown off their feet, vegetables rolled off their stands, and hats landed on the wrong heads. Encourage students to look at the humorous effects that a big wind could have. Generate some ideas orally. Then give each child a sheet of lined paper to write a paragraph or short story about "The Big Wind." Follow up by inviting children to illustrate their stories. Combine the stories and illustrations in a class book entitled "The Big Wind Comes to (name of your town or city)." Children might also enjoy hearing the story *Iva Dunnit and the Big Wind* by Carol Purdy.

The Hat Parade
Art

The people in the story ended up with different hats because the wind mixed them all up in the air. Children can have fun with a mixed-up hat parade of their own. Reproduce a copy of "The Hat Parade" on page 24 for each child. Use an X-acto knife to cut the slits on each sheet before distributing them to the children. Give each child a 2" x 22" strip of white paper. Children slip the strip through the slits so that it slides across the paper. Then the children position the strip in one place and draw a hat over each person's head. When all three hats are drawn, children can slide the strip and reposition it so that they can draw a different set of three hats over the people's heads. When the strip is covered with interesting hats, the children can have fun sliding the strip and matching or mismatching hats with heads! Add to the fun by having each child make a hat to wear. *Hats, Hats, and More Hats!* by Jean Stangl (Fearon Teacher Aids, 1989) is an excellent resource with simple patterns for making a wide variety of hats. January 20 is National Hat Day. If possible, celebrate the day by having children come to school wearing a unique handmade hat. Have a hat parade around the school.

Wind-Powered Puffs
Science

Discuss ways in which the wind is helpful to us and how we use the wind to help us accomplish tasks. For example, we use blow dryers, clothes dryers, fans, and we even blow on hot food to cool it before we eat it. Encourage children to think of other ways to use wind. Invite children to use their wind power to accomplish a task. Divide the class into four or five equal teams. Have one person from each team kneel behind a starting line. Place a cotton ball in front of each person. On the start signal, students blow the cotton balls across the finish line about 6 feet away. Repeat until each student has had a turn. After the relay, discuss some of the problems with wind power, such as harnessing the energy and controlling its effects.

Wind-Powered Rocket
Science

Show children a picture of a wind turbine and explain how wind can help generate power that can be used to create energy. Demonstrate how to build a wind-powered rocket with the following instructions:

1. Stretch a string tightly from one side of the room to the other.
2. Thread the string through a plastic drinking straw.
3. Blow up a balloon and hold the end with your finger to prevent the air from escaping.
4. Using tape, attach the balloon to the underside of the straw.
5. Let the air out of the balloon and watch the "rocket" fly across the room on the string.

Give each child a plastic drinking straw and a balloon. Have children work in pairs to stretch a string between two points and launch their rockets. After children have had a chance to experiment, discuss the scientific principle of wind-powered propulsion.

The Hat Parade

Slip the paper strip through the slits. Draw some interesting hats on the strip. Have fun sliding the strip and matching heads and hats.

cut slit

Clouds, Rain, Wind, and Snow © 1991 Fearon Teacher Aids

Hide and Seek Fog

Written by Alvin Tresselt and illustrated by Roger Duvoisin
New York: Lothrop, Lee & Shepard, 1965

Synopsis

The worst fog in twenty years rolls into a small coastal village. The lobster-men patiently wait three days for a clearing. The children find the fog to be a natural camouflage for a great game of hide-and-seek.

Introduction

Show the children the cover of the book and ask them to describe what is happening in the picture. Ask the children why they think the artist drew the picture in an unclear way. Invite children to listen closely as the story is read aloud to find out how the fog affects the people living in a small village.

Critical-Thinking and Discussion Questions

1. When the lobsterman first saw the fog, he knew he would have to take his boat back to shore. Why do you think he couldn't stay out and continue setting his lobster pots? Do all ships and boats have to dock when fog rolls in? Why or why not?
2. The weather changed the plans of the village people. They could not do the things they normally did. Has weather ever affected your plans? When? What did you do?
3. The lobstermen were impatiently waiting for the fog to lift so that they could take their boats out to set lobster pots and to fish. How did the men spend the time during those three foggy days? Do you think they wasted their time or made good use of it? Why? What do you do when you have to wait for something or someone?
4. Some village people scowled and complained because the fog upset their plans, and others tried to cheer everyone else up. How do you usually react when something doesn't happen the way you wanted it to?
5. Do you think this story could really happen? Why or why not? Where do you think this village might be located?

Creative Writing Starters
Language Arts

On a foggy day, I like to _____ .
I had to change my plans when _____ .
Fog reminds me of _____ .

Story Titles
Hide and Seek Happiness
Weather Worries
Fog Frolic

Fog Cinquain
Language Arts

The author described the fog in many ways to help the reader visualize what it looked like and how it felt. For example, the author said, " . . . the fog twisted about the cottages like slow-motion smoke." He described the fog as "damp cotton wool." The author even described the movement of the fog by saying that it hid the town and "tip-toed past the windows." Point out the author's excellent use of descriptive words to the children. Explain the elements of a cinquain:

first line—one-word title
second line—two words describing the title
third line—three words telling about the action of the title
fourth line—four words telling about the author's feelings about the title
fifth line—one word restating the title

Practice writing a cinquain together as a class. Give each child a copy of the "Fog Cinquain" reproducible on page 29. Encourage children to write their own original fog cinquains.

Party Plans

Language Arts

Have students think of some possible outdoor parties and make a list on the chalkboard (beach party, barbeque, picnic). Challenge students to imagine that they have planned to have one of these outdoor parties, and at the last minute, some weather changes have made the party impossible. Have students brainstorm some indoor-activity alternatives. After the class has generated some ideas, divide students into groups of four or five and give each group a copy of the "Change in Plans" reproducible on page 30. Have each group plan an outdoor party and an indoor alternative.

As Thick as Pea Soup

Language Arts

Pea Soup and Sea Serpents, by William Schroder, is an amusing book about two boys who decide to hunt for sea serpents on a foggy day in a nearby pond. The fog is as thick as pea soup, but the boys consider that to be an advantage—they can take the monster by surprise. The boys never realize that the fog can be an advantage for the monster as well. Read the book aloud to the children. After reading the book, ask the children to speculate how the story would have been different if the fog had lifted and the boys had been able to see what was happening. Ask the children how the actions and reactions of Norton, Atherton, and the sea serpent might have changed.

Foggy Fun

Art

Have each child make a crayon drawing depicting some scene or event in *Hide and Seek Fog*. Children can add a gray wash by using diluted gray tempera paint to give the picture a foggy appearance.

Name _____

Fog Cinquain

_____

(1-word title)

_____

(2 words to describe the title)

_____

(3 words to describe the action of the title)

_____

(4 words describing your feelings about the title)

_____

(1 word renaming the title)

Clouds, Rain, Wind, and Snow © 1991 Fearon Teacher Aids

Change in Plans

Plan an outdoor party. Also plan an indoor party in case the weather causes a change in plans.

	OUTDOOR PARTY	INDOOR PARTY
Kind of Party		
Time and Date		
Place		
Food		
Decorations		
Games		

Clouds, Rain, Wind, and Snow © 1991 Fearon Teacher Aids

The Storm Book

Written by Charlotte Zolotow and illustrated by Margaret Bloy Graham
New York: Harper & Brothers, 1952

Synopsis

The author uses vividly descriptive language to carry the reader through the rise and fall of a summer storm. The day begins hot and still and slowly builds to a storm-darkened sky with starlight flashes of lightning and the sound of rolling thunder. After the storm has climaxed, the calm once again returns, marked by a beautiful rainbow.

Introduction

Show children the first picture in the book and ask them to describe what they see. Encourage children to think about what would be different in the picture if there were a storm. Invite children to listen closely as the story is read aloud and to look carefully at the illustrations so that they will notice all the details of the storm the author describes.

Critical-Thinking and Discussion Questions

1. As the boy was lying in the field, he began to notice some changes in the weather. What are some things you notice when a storm is approaching?
2. The story tells how the effects of the storm vary in the country, the city, the seashore, and the mountains. In which of those places have you been during a rainstorm? What are some things you noticed happening while it was raining?
3. The little boy was curious about the lightning and thunder. He asked his mother to explain what was happening. How do you think he was feeling? Have you ever seen lightning or heard thunder? Does it frighten you? Should it? Do you think either of those things can hurt you?
4. Where do you think is the best place to be during a storm? Where would you *not* like to be during a storm? Why?
5. A beautiful rainbow appeared after the storm. Have you ever seen a rainbow? What did it look like? Do you remember what colors you saw in it?

Creative Writing Starters
Language Arts

Roaring thunder makes me feel _____ .
When it rains I can look out my window and see _____ .
The best part about a rainstorm is _____ .

Story Titles
The Crash of Thunder
All Is Still
Over the Rainbow

Storm Sequence
Language Arts

This story strongly shows the progression of the storm building to a climax. Point out the definite beginning, middle, and end of the story and explain why these are important elements in all stories. Give each child a 9" x 12" sheet of white construction paper. Tell the children to cut the paper into fourths and draw a picture on each section to portray a part of the story. Encourage children to include a picture that represents the beginning of the story, two to represent the storm in the middle of the story, and to have the last picture represent the end of the story. Give each child a 12" x 18" sheet of light-colored construction paper. Have children glue the four sections in order on the large sheet of paper. Invite children to give the large sheet of paper a title and then write a descriptive sentence at the bottom of each picture to describe the illustrations.

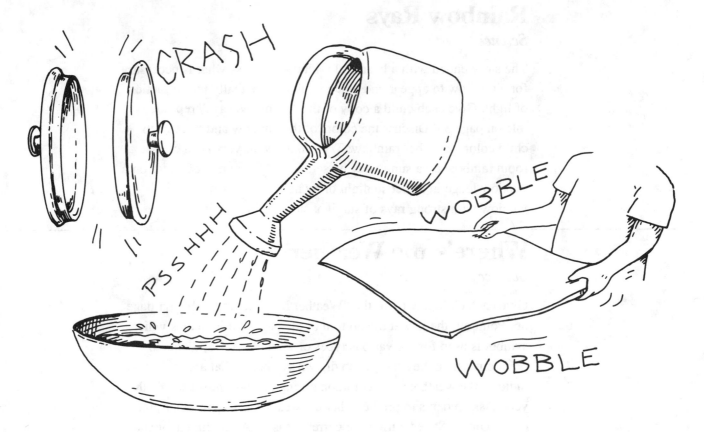

Storm Symphony

Music and Language Arts

Read the story again and encourage children to listen carefully for all descriptions of the sights and sounds of the storm. Have children point them out as you read. Stop reading as the sights and sounds are identified and make a list on the chalkboard. Your list may include the following:

    cool wind begins to blow
    thunder begins to roll
    lightning flashes
    rain falls
    automobiles pass, making swish-swishing sounds
    terrible beating sound of rain and wind splattering
    pitpatpitpatting

Discuss some ways that these sounds could be reproduced in the classroom. Ask children how they think they could imitate the sound of thunder or the sound of automobiles driving on wet streets. Also point out that silence precedes and follows the noisy storm. After generating some ideas, divide the class into groups of four or five and have each group work together to create a storm, using sound effects. Children may think of props they would like to bring from home. Plan to have the groups perform their storm symphonies the following day for the class.

Rainbow Rays

Science

The story ended with a beautiful rainbow. Discuss what is necessary for a rainbow to appear and that a rainbow is actually the refraction of light. Give each child a copy of the "Rainbow Rays" reproducible on page 35. Discuss the colors of the rainbow and have each child color his or her rainbow. Try making your very own classroom rainbow on a sunny day by setting a shallow pan of water on a window ledge in direct sunlight or by holding a prism up to a window with strong rays of sunlight shining through it.

Where's the Weather?

Science

Give each child a copy of the "Weather Map" reproducible on page 36. Point out the key at the bottom of the page that indicates which symbol is used for the various types of weather. Ask students to point out where they live. Then draw a symbol in that area to indicate the weather most common during the current season of the year. Ask students to predict what the weather is like in other places of the United States during the current season. After students make predictions, help children fill in symbols in other places on the map to indicate accurate information.

Name _____

Rainbow Rays

Each rainbow is an arc of bands the color of the spectrum. Start with the top band and color your rainbow red, orange, yellow, green, blue, and violet.

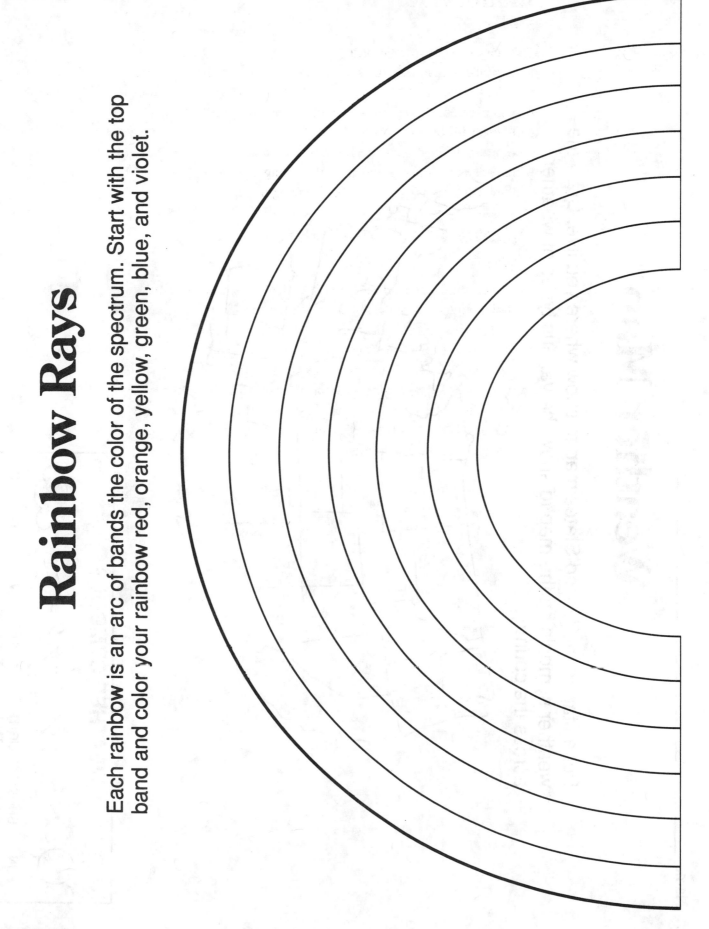

Weather Map

Put a star on the United States map to show where you live. Draw the weather symbols on the map to show the various types of weather across the country.

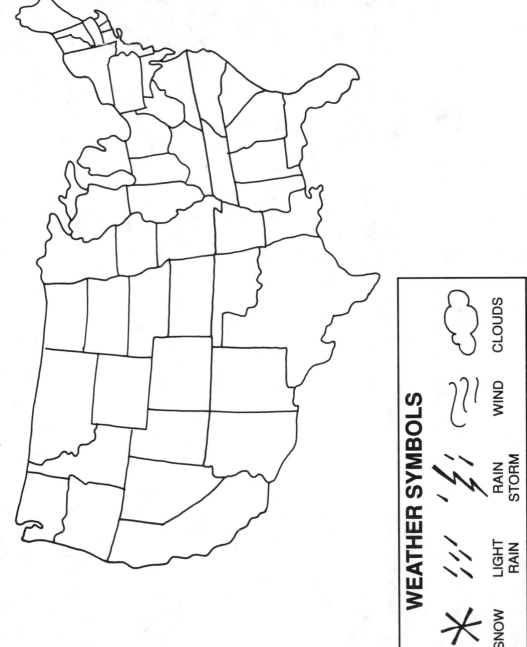

WEATHER SYMBOLS

| SUN | SNOW | LIGHT RAIN | RAIN STORM | WIND | CLOUDS |

Peter Spier's Rain

Illustrated by Peter Spier
New York: Doubleday, 1982

Synopsis

This wordless book cleverly illustrates the journey of two children exploring their neighborhood during a downpour. The children splash through puddles, make footprints in the mud, and duck under drainpipes. When the wind begins to pick up, they rush home where it is cozy and warm.

Introduction

Ask children to think about the kind of fun they could have if they could play outdoors in the rain. Ask them what they would like to do. Ask children to think about what they would wear to keep from getting too wet and cold. Invite the children to look closely at the pictures in this wordless book to find out what the characters in the story do and what they wear in the rain. This book is best shown in a small group, so that everyone can see the pictures clearly.

Critical-Thinking and Discussion Questions

1. The children's mother allowed them to go back outside and play in the rain after they put on their slickers and rubber boots. Do you think that was a good idea? Why or why not?
2. Have you ever played outside in the rain? Did you do any of the same things the children in the story did? What did you do?
3. Many of the animals in the story were looking for a place to hide. Can you remember some of the animals and the places they hid? If you were outside in your yard when it began to rain and you could not go inside, where would you hide to keep dry?
4. Why do you think the children had to take a bath when they came in the house out of the rain?
5. (Show the children the last picture in the book.) Look at the picture carefully. Do you think the rain did any damage to the children's backyard? What do you think it might have ruined? Can you think of some ways that the rain was helpful?

Creative Writing Starters
Language Arts

On a rainy day, I _____ .
When I see a puddle, I _____ .
The next time it rains, I want to _____ .

Story Titles
A Walk in the Rain
My Broken Umbrella
Splish, Splash

Circle Stories
Language Arts

Invite the children to sit in a circle. Give one child *Peter Spier's Rain*. Encourage the child to look at the first picture and say a sentence or two to describe what is happening in that picture. Pass the book to the next child to describe the next picture. Continue around the circle until each child has had a turn to add words to the detailed illustrations.

Pop-Up Umbrella
Art

Give each child a copy of the umbrella pattern reproducible on page 40 and an 8¹/₂" x 11" sheet of white drawing paper. Have children cut out the umbrella and handle patterns. Have the children fold the umbrella pattern in half on the dotted line. Fold the triangular corner down on the dotted line. Unfold the triangle and cut the umbrella scallops. Unfold the umbrella and glue it to a sheet of drawing paper with glue on the back of the areas that are shaded in diagram 5 on the reproducible. The umbrella handle can be glued to the bottom of the pop-up portion. Children can decorate their pictures to make a rainy day scene.

Making Rain
Science

You can make rain by using a cup of water, a glass coffee pot, ice cubes, and a saucer. Put the water in the coffee pot. Cover the coffee pot with a saucer filled with ice cubes. Warm the water over a low heat. The warm air in the coffee pot cools when it nears the saucer filled with ice cubes and condenses to form water droplets. The droplets will fall like rain off the saucer into the water below.

Absorb or Repel
Science

In the story, the rain showers down on everything, including the clothes hanging on the clothesline, the dog, the ducks in the pond, and even the children. Ask the students to explain why the children in the story put on special clothes before they went outside in the rain. If you have a vinyl raincoat, show it to the children and explain that the fabric it is made of repels water. Explain the meaning of the words *absorb* and *repel*. Ask children to find a partner. Give each pair a cupful of water, a medicine dropper, and the following list of materials:

> small container of sand
> small square of waxed paper
> small square of cotton fabric
> a leaf
> small square of construction paper

Children can use the medicine dropper to drop water on each item in the list of materials to determine whether each item absorbs or repels water.

1.

2.

3.

4.

5.

Cut here.

40

Peter Spier's Rain

The Cloud Book

Written and illustrated by Tomie de Paola
New York: Holiday House, 1975

Synopsis

This informational book presents the ten most common types of clouds. Clever illustrations explain each cloud's shape and nickname. Myths and weather predictions based on clouds are also explained.

Introduction

Give several children a cotton ball and ask them to stretch and pull the cotton ball to make it look like a cloud. Each child may come up with a different-looking cloud. Ask children if clouds can come in different shapes or colors. Encourage children to listen closely as the story is read aloud to find out about the different shapes and colors of clouds and to see whether clouds can tell us anything about the weather.

Critical-Thinking and Discussion Questions

1. The book said that almost anytime you go outside, you can see clouds. Can you ever remember looking up at the sky and not seeing any clouds? What do you think the weather would be like on a day when there were no clouds? Is it possible for rain to fall if there are no clouds in the sky?
2. Have you ever flown in an airplane? Did you see any clouds when you were up in the air? What did they look like? How did they look as the airplane passed through them?
3. Fog is a cloud that is very low to the ground. The book said that fog can come right into your front yard. Do you think it is possible for fog to come in your house? Why or why not?
4. Many people look at clouds and think that the shapes remind them of something else. Have you ever thought a cloud looked like something else? What?
5. What kind of clouds do you most often see in the sky? Which clouds are your favorites? Why?

Creative Writing Starters
Language Arts

Once I thought a cloud looked like a _____ .
Some clouds remind me of _____.
My favorite kind of clouds are the ones that look like _____ .

Story Titles
The Cloudless Day
The Mysterious Cloud
Lost in the Fog

The Cloud Story
Language Arts

Give each student a 9" x 12" sheet of white construction paper and several cotton balls. Have each student fold the sheet of construction paper into fourths to make four frames for a cloud story. Encourage students to make a silly, four-frame story about a cloud as the author did at the end of *The Cloud Book*. Invite students to draw illustrations and write a line or phrase of text in each frame. Have students glue the cotton balls to the illustrations to represent the clouds.

① Once there was a cloud

② Who married another cloud

③ And had a lot of baby clouds.

④ They started a family business making rain.

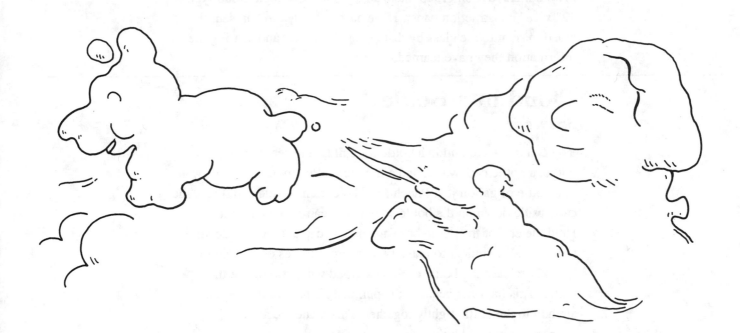

It Looked Like . . .
Art

Read *It Looked Like Spilt Milk* by Charles G. Shaw. The author takes a closer look at clouds and sees other shapes, such as a flower, an angel, and a great horned owl. Give each child a 9" x 12" sheet of white and a 9" x 12" sheet of blue construction paper. Have the children tear the white sheet into the shape of some object and glue it in the center of the blue sheet of construction paper. Each child writes what his or her torn cloud looks like at the bottom of the page. Combine all the pages together in a class book called "It Looked Like . . . ." Add a page at the end of the book that says, "But it was just a cloud in the sky." Encourage children to take a closer look at the real clouds in the sky the next time they are outdoors to see if they notice some familiar shapes.

Cloud Clubs
Science

Divide the class into groups of three to form "cloud clubs." Assign each "club" a different type of cloud as their club mascot.

cirrus	cirrostratus	nimbostratus
cumulus	altostratus	stratocumulus
stratus	altocumulus	cumulonimbus
cirrocumulus		

Invite groups to gather as much information as possible about their type of cloud, using *The Cloud Book* and other sources as reference material. Have each group make a large poster of their cloud type on 12" x 18" construction paper. Have each "cloud club" present their cloud mascot to the class by displaying the poster and sharing the information they have learned.

Cloud in a Bottle
Science

You can make a cloud in a bottle for children to see by using a bottle, a bottle cap, water, and a tire pump. Put about $1/2$ cup of water in a bottle or gallon jug. Punch a $1/4$" hole in the bottle cap. Place the cap upside down on the bottle so that you can remove it quickly. Hold the end of the pump hose against the cap and push it down tightly. Ask a student to make two or three strokes on the pump. Quickly release the bottle cap and a cloud will form inside the bottle. This happens because the pumped air pushed the air that was already in the bottle tightly together. This made the air a little warmer, so it could hold more water vapor. When you released the cap, the air spread out again and cooled. The cooler air could not hold as much water vapor, so droplets formed. A cloud is made of water droplets that are held in the air. (Read *It's Raining Cats and Dogs* by Franklyn M. Branley, 1987.)

Umbrella

Written by Taro Yashima
New York: Viking Press, 1958

Synopsis

Momo is a young Japanese-American girl who receives an umbrella for her third birthday. She is so excited to use her new umbrella, but she must wait for rain. Children will relate to Momo's impatience and the pride Momo feels when she finally gets to walk home from nursery school, using her new umbrella.

Introduction

Put an umbrella in a paper sack ahead of time. Show children the sack and explain that you have something very special inside. Build the suspense by giving some clues. Then ask children how they would feel if they had to wait until tomorrow to find out what was inside the sack. Point out how hard it is to wait for something. Open the bag and show them the umbrella. The story is about a little girl who receives an umbrella and is very impatient while waiting to use it, just as the children were impatient about wanting to know what was inside the bag. Encourage children to listen closely as the story is read aloud to find out if Momo ever gets to use her new umbrella.

Critical-Thinking and Discussion Questions

1. Momo was so pleased with her new red rubber boots and umbrella that she got up in the middle of the night to look at them. Have you ever been that excited about a gift you received? What was it?
2. Momo began thinking of other uses for her umbrella besides keeping herself dry from the rain. Can you think of some other ways to use an umbrella?
3. Momo reminded herself that although the rainy streets were crowded and noisy, she must walk straight "like a grown-up lady." What do you think she meant by that? Have you ever tried to act grown-up? What did you do?
4. Momo thought the raindrops that fell on the umbrella made wonderful music. What sounds did Momo think the raindrops made? What sounds do you think the rain makes when it hits your umbrella?
5. Momo often forgot to take her things home with her from nursery school. But she did not forget her umbrella. Why do you think she remembered her umbrella? What do you think would have happened if she had forgotten it? Do you ever forget things?

Creative Writing Starters
Language Arts

My favorite birthday present was _____ .
I don't like to wait for _____ .
Sometimes I forget to _____ .
I remember the first time I _____ .

Story Titles
I Could Hardly Wait
All by Myself
The Best Rainy Day

Japanese Characters
Language Arts

Point out the Japanese characters in the story for the seasons of the year. Explain to children that Japanese is not written with the same symbols we use when we write. Give each child a copy of the "Japanese Characters" reproducible on page 48, a sheet of thin drawing paper, and a black crayon. Have children lay the thin drawing paper over the reproducible and trace the Japanese characters. Some children may want to try to draw the characters without tracing.

Rain Music
Art and Music

This activity is especially fun to do on a rainy day. Give each child an empty oatmeal container without the lid and a 7" x 14" sheet of construction paper. Ask children to decorate the sheets of construction paper and then glue the sheets around their oatmeal containers to make decorative drums. Encourage children to listen to the sound of the rain hitting the roof or sidewalk and to pound out a rhythm on their drums to imitate the sounds they hear. To incorporate some listening and sequencing practice, pound out a short rhythm on your drum and have children repeat the rhythm back to you.

Chalk Pictures
Art

The pictures Momo had drawn on the sidewalk with chalk had washed away when the raindrops hit them. Give children the opportunity to see how water can affect their chalk drawings. Give each child a sheet of white drawing paper and colored chalk to draw a picture. When the pictures are complete, pass around several spray bottles filled with water. Invite children to spray their pictures with water and to watch how the pictures change.

Raindrop Size
Science

Rain comes from clouds, which are made of droplets of water. Each raindrop contains millions of tiny droplets. There are several ways to actually measure the size of a single raindrop. When raindrops first begin to fall, the students can see them splash on the dry sidewalk. Or set out a piece of cardboard or construction paper to catch the first drops of rain. Another method is to stretch a piece of nylon stocking over the top of a can. Cover the stretched nylon with a thin layer of powdered sugar. Put the can or box in the rain for a few seconds. The raindrops will dissolve the sugar and leave a spot where they go through the nylon. (Read *It's Raining Cats and Dogs* by Franklyn M. Branley, 1987.)

Japanese Characters

Japanese words are not written with the same letters we use. Try writing these Japanese words. Lay a thin sheet of paper over this page. Use a black crayon to trace the characters.

Momo (Peach)

Ame (rain)

Natsu (summer)

Haru (spring)

Clouds, Rain, Wind, and Snow © 1991 Fearon Teacher Aids

Umbrella

Mushroom in the Rain

Adapted by Mirra Ginsburg
and illustrated by Jose Aruego and Ariane Dewey
New York: Macmillan, 1974

Synopsis

An ant finds shelter from the rain under a mushroom that appears to be just big enough for him. But soon a butterfly, mouse, sparrow, and rabbit all join him under the tiny mushroom. The animals are amazed at how there always seems to be room for one more. The wise old frog explains why.

Introduction

Show children a mushroom and ask them to tell you all they know about it. Ask children if they know what happens to mushrooms in the rain. Explain that the answer to that question is the secret to the story, *Mushroom in the Rain*. Encourage children to listen closely as the story is read aloud to find out the secret.

Critical-Thinking and Discussion Questions

1. When the ant was caught in the rain, he chose to hide under a mushroom. Where would you hide if you were outside when it began to rain?
2. Do you think this story is real or make-believe? Why?
3. What do you think would have happened to the butterfly, the mouse, the sparrow, and the rabbit if the ant had not shared the shelter of the mushroom with them? What are some things you share with others? How do you feel when someone refuses to share with you?
4. Why did the animals refuse to let the fox hide under the mushroom? Do you think they were fair? Do you think he would have fit?
5. The frog seemed to be very wise. He knew that the mushroom was able to shelter all the animals. What other animals are often considered wise? Do you consider yourself wise? Why or why not?

Creative Writing Starters
Language Arts

One time I tried to hide under a _____ .
When it rains I usually _____ .
I like to share my _____ .

Story Titles
The Giant Mushroom
Room for One More
The Best Hiding Place

Just Like Me
Language Arts

Discuss the characteristics of each animal:

The frog seemed to be very wise. He knew answers that nobody else seemed to know.

The ant was generous because he allowed all the other animals to join him under the mushroom.

The rabbit was frightened because the fox was chasing him.

Have students choose one of the characters they think is most like them and orally or on paper tell why by completing the following sentence:

I am most like the _____ because I _____ .

Mushrooms, Umbrellas, and More!
Art

Cut several 6" circles from tagboard. Cut the circles in half and give each student a half circle. Ask students if they noticed anything in the story that had this half-circle shape (mushroom tops). Point out that an umbrella is the same shape. Ask students to think about other things that are this shape. Invite students to trace the half-circle shape on a sheet of drawing paper and then to turn the shape into a picture. The half circle can be a mouse, a turtle shell, or the bottom of a sailboat. Combine all the pictures together in a class book entitled "Mushrooms, Umbrellas, and More!"

Stuffed Mushrooms
Cooking and Health

Show children a fresh mushroom. Caution children that picking fresh mushrooms from a yard and eating them can be dangerous because some mushrooms are poisonous. It is safest to purchase fresh mushrooms from the store. Canned mushrooms can also be purchased. Ask children if they have ever eaten mushrooms, and if so, how the mushrooms were prepared. Invite children to help you prepare "Stuffed Mushrooms" from the following recipe:

> To make the filling, combine:
> 4 $\frac{1}{2}$ oz cream cheese
> $\frac{1}{2}$ tsp worcestershire sauce
> dash pepper
> 1 T mayonnaise

Add grated cheddar cheese and fine bread crumbs until the mixture is a stirrable consistency. Decap large mushrooms and scoop out the caps to form a little cup. Stuff each mushroom with the filling. Place on a baking sheet and bake at 350° for 15 minutes or until heated through. Serve warm.

Mushroom Madness
Math

Give each student a copy of the "Mushroom Madness" reproducible on page 52. Have students read the problems carefully and then calculate the answers. When the problems have all been solved, invite students to turn the paper over and write an original story problem on the back. Collect the papers and read some of the original problems aloud for the class to solve.

Mushroom Madness

Read each problem carefully and then write the answers on the lines.

1. The ant was alone under the mushroom. The butterfly, mouse, sparrow, and rabbit joined him. How many animals were under the mushroom all together? _____

2. The mushroom was 2 inches tall before it started raining. The mushroom was 6 inches tall after the rain. How many inches did the mushroom grow? _____

3. It started raining at 9:00 in the morning. The rain stopped at noon. How many hours did it rain? _____

4. The mouse was 4 inches long. The rabbit was 3 times longer. How long was the rabbit? _____

5. The ant was only half as long as the mouse. The mouse was 4 inches long. How long was the ant? _____

6. There were 9 mushrooms growing in the yard before the rain. After several days, the owl noticed that there were 14 mushrooms. How many more mushrooms had grown? _____

7. If 5 animals can hide under one mushroom, how many animals can hide under 3 mushrooms? _____

Write a story problem of your own on the back of your paper.

Clouds, Rain, Wind, and Snow © 1991 Fearon Teacher Aids

Mushroom in the Rain

Bringing the Rain to Kapiti Plain

Retold by Verna Aardema and illustrated by Beatriz Vidal
New York: Dial Press, 1981

Synopsis

This African tale is a cumulative rhyme, much like "The House That Jack Built." A drought prompts Ki-Pat to shoot an arrow into the big, black cloud that shadows the ground and brings rain to Kapiti Plain. The rain "greens up" the grass and provides food for Ki-Pat's cows.

Introduction

Show children the cover of *Bringing the Rain to Kapiti Plain* and ask them where they think the story takes place. Point out Africa on a world map and its distance from where you live. After reading the title of the book to the children, ask them if they think it is possible to "bring rain." Encourage children to listen carefully as the story is read aloud to find out how the rain was brought to the plain. Children will enjoy "reading" the repetitive phrases along with you as they become familiar with the pattern.

Critical-Thinking and Discussion Questions

1. Do you think this story is real or make-believe? Why?
2. Ki-Pat was able to change the weather by shooting an arrow into the dark cloud. Do you think it is really possible to change the weather? If you could order a specific kind of weather, what kind of weather would you want? Why?
3. Ki-Pat helped to end the drought. What is a drought? How would you be affected if there were a drought here? Would your life be different? In what ways?
4. Why do you think Ki-Pat stood on one leg like a big stork bird?
5. Do you think there will be another drought on Kapiti Plain? Why or why not? What do you think Ki-Pat would do if there were?
6. Do you think it is possible to ever have too much water? If not having enough water is called a drought, what would having too much water be called? Which would you rather have? Why?

Creative Writing Starters
Language Arts

If there were a drought where I live, I would _____.
Rain is helpful because it _____.
I especially like the weather when it is _____.

Story Titles
Big Black Cloud
Bull's-Eye
The Rainmaker

Going on a Picnic
Language Arts

This is a great game to improve memory and sequencing skills. Have children sit in a circle. Explain to the children that they will all be going on an imaginary picnic. Ask each child to think of something that he or she would like to take along on the picnic, beginning with the first letter of his or her name. For example, Carol might like to take cookies, Judy can take jellybeans, and Tom can take tomatoes. Have the first child repeat the following sentence aloud and fill in the blanks:

"My name is _____ and I am taking _____ to the picnic."

Have the second child repeat the first child's name and what he or she is taking and then repeat the sentence and fill in the blanks with his or her own name and choice. Have the third child repeat what the first two children are taking and then repeat the sentence with his or her name and choice. Continue around the circle, having each child repeat what the others have said and then adding his or her own picnic item. You can be the last person in the circle with the hardest job of repeating each child's name and picnic item.

Rhyming Pairs
Language Arts

This story has excellent rhythm and rhyme and is fun to read aloud. Read through the book again. Ask children to point out the pairs of rhyming words and make a list of them on the chalkboard. Review the words together and be sure children are able to read each of them. Have children choose a partner. Give each pair a copy of the "Rhyming Pairs" reproducible on page 56. Invite each pair to cut apart the word cards. Have one partner match the rhyming words as quickly as possible and have the other partner check for accuracy. Mix the word cards up and give the other partner a chance to make the matches. The word cards can also be used for a game of "Rhyming Concentration" or to make rhyming word booklets.

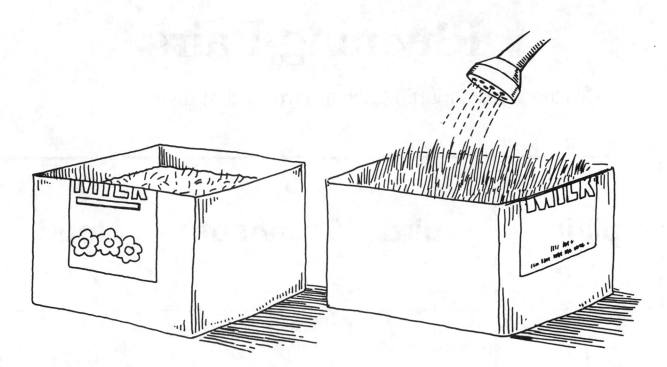

Drought Dangers
Science

The drought in the story caused the grass to become brown and die. Conduct the following experiment to show the children what that grass may have looked like. Fill two ½ gallon milk cartons that have been cut down to about 6" with potting soil. Plant some grass seed in both cartons and water both equally until the grass has sprouted. Continue to water one carton and let the other carton dry out. Discuss the results of the experiment and how drought conditions affect other living things. After the grass has turned brown, try watering it to see if it will become green again.

Weather Predictions
Science

In the story, Ki-Pat tried to change the weather because rain was so desperately needed. Ki-Pat had no way of knowing if rain would be falling soon or not, and he could not wait. Long ago, people did not have radios, television sets, newspapers, or meteorologists to give them a weather forecast. So people would often look at the color of the sky, the shape of the clouds, the behavior of animals, or the sun and moon to try to predict the weather. *A January Fog Will Freeze a Hog,* compiled and edited by Hubert Davis, is a collection of weather folklore. Each of the thirty ditties is accompanied by an explanation of the scientific basis for the saying. Share some of the sayings with the children and then discuss whether Ki-Pat could have used any of these signs to predict the next rainfall.

Rhyming Pairs

Cut the words apart. Match the words that rhyme.

plain	bird	about	loud
weather	dead	dry	thong
strong	sky	rain	belated
cloud	herd	overhead	Ki-Pat
drought	fat	migrated	feather

Bringing the Rain to Kapiti Plain

Rain & Hail

Written by Franklyn M. Branley and illustrated by Harriett Barton
New York: Thomas Y. Crowell, 1963

Synopsis

A simply written, informative book about rain and hail. The text traces the water cycle, including explanations about why water evaporates, how clouds form, and how and why the water droplets fall back to the ground.

Introduction

Show children a golfball and ask them what they would do if something that size started falling from the sky. Ask them if they think raindrops or snowflakes could ever be that large. Show children a softball and ask the same questions. Encourage children to listen closely as the story is read aloud to find out about the day that something as large as a softball did fall from the sky.

Critical-Thinking and Discussion Questions

1. Have you ever "seen your breath"? Why are you able to see it sometimes and not able to see it at other times?
2. Can raindrops be different sizes? Why or why not?
3. Now that you know what causes rain and hail, do you think it is possible for both rain and hail to fall from the sky at the same time? Why or why not?
4. If you had been in Kansas in 1970 when hailstones as big as softballs fell, what would you have done? The cornfields were flattened by the huge hailstones. What other damage might have occurred? How long do you think it took for those hailstones to melt?
5. Water evaporates into the air and forms clouds. When the clouds can no longer hold all the water, rain falls. After the rain falls to the ground, the water evaporates into the air again, forms clouds, and then rain falls again. This is called a cycle because it keeps happening over and over. Can you think of other cycles in nature that happen over and over again?

Creative Writing Starters
Language Arts

I would like to catch a hailstone as big as a _____ .
My favorite kind of cloud is _____ .
Once when it was raining, I _____ .

Story Titles
The Rowdy Raindrop
The Biggest Cloudburst Ever
The Case of the Vanishing Vapor

Weather Riddles
Language Arts

Give students an opportunity to use the knowledge they have gained from the story to write original weather riddles. Practice writing a few as a class to help generate some ideas. Students can write riddles in prose or poetry couplets.

I collect in the clouds,
and can't wait to fall down.
When the clouds get too full,
I fall to the ground.
What am I?
(Raindrop)

I can appear in all sizes,
As big as a softball it is said.
I freeze before I fall.
Look out! I may hit your head.
What am I?
(Hail)

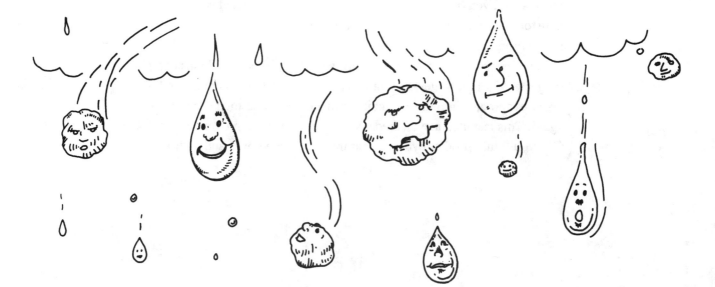

Raindrop Art
Art

Give each child a raindrop-shaped pattern cut from tagboard and a sheet of white drawing paper. Invite children to use their pencils and trace the raindrop pattern over and over onto their papers to make interesting raindrop designs. After the design is completed, encourage students to use crayons, markers, or paint to add color.

The Water Cycle
Science

Give each child a copy of "The Water Cycle" reproducible on page 60. Discuss the water cycle and be sure to include and explain the three words listed at the bottom of the reproducible.

> Heat from the sun causes water to evaporate into the air in the form of water vapor. When the air cools, the water vapor condenses into droplets of water that form clouds. The droplets combine with other droplets to produce precipitation that falls to the ground in the form of rain, snow, or hail. This evaporation, condensation, precipitation cycle is repeated over and over.

Invite children to cut the words apart and glue them in the boxes to correctly label the water cycle. Children can color the picture after the labels are in place.

Evaporation Race
Science

Conduct an evaporation experiment with the class. Pour $1/4$ cup of water in a large pan. Put some soil in another pan and add $1/4$ cup water. Put a piece of fabric in a third pan and add $1/4$ cup water. Place the three pans out in the sun. Ask children to predict how long it will take for the water to evaporate from each pan and why. Have children observe the three pans at 1-hour intervals. After completing the experiment, discuss the results and how they compare to the children's predictions.

The Water Cycle

Cut the worksheet apart on the dotted line. Cut the words apart.
Glue the words in the correct boxes to label the water cycle. Color
your picture.

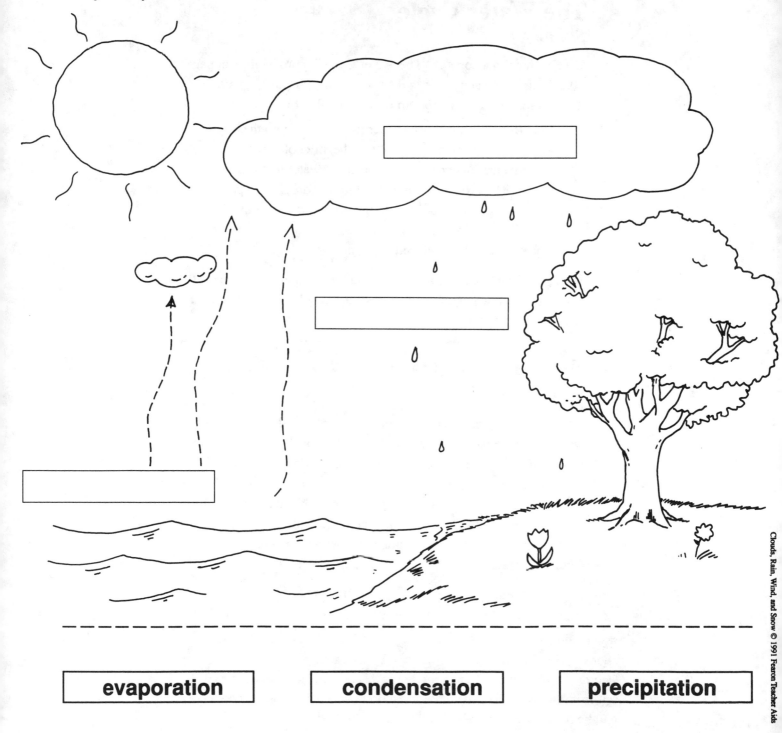

| evaporation | condensation | precipitation |

Cloudy with a Chance of Meatballs

Written by Judi Barrett and illustrated by Ron Barrett
New York: Atheneum, 1980

Synopsis

Grandpa tells a tall tale of a land called Chewandswallow, where food arrives in the form of weather. In Chewandswallow it rains soup and juice, snows mashed potatoes, and frankfurters blow in from the northwest. The people are very satisfied until violent storms bring an overabundance of food.

Introduction

Ask the children to name some things that fall from the sky. They will probably name forms of weather such as rain, hail, snow, or sleet. Remind children of the saying "It's raining cats and dogs." Ask them what it would be like if cats and dogs really did fall from the sky. In the story, *Cloudy with a Chance of Meatballs,* something very unusual falls from the sky. Encourage children to listen closely as the story is read aloud to find out what falls from the sky.

Critical-Thinking and Discussion Questions

1. What are some of the advantages and disadvantages of living in the town of Chewandswallow? Would you like to live there? Why or why not?
2. The children's grandpa didn't explain in his story why there was a sudden turn of events in the weather. Why do you think awful things began happening? Do you think there was anything the people of Chewandswallow could have done besides run away? What would you have done?
3. Nobody dared to return to Chewandswallow. Would you have been brave enough to return? What do you think you would have seen?
4. Show the children the picture of the children sledding with their grandpa at the end of the book. Why do you think the children thought they saw a giant pat of butter and could smell mashed potatoes? What did they really see?
5. If you could choose any kind of food to fall from the sky, what would you choose? How could you store the food if too much fell?
6. One day, Gorgonzola cheese, overcooked broccoli, and brussel sprouts fell from the sky. The people did not enjoy those foods. What food would you be dissatisfied with if it fell from the sky?

Creative Writing Starters
Language Arts

I would/would not like to live in Chewandswallow because _____.

I would love it if _____ fell from the sky.

_____ would be a real problem if food fell from the sky.

Story Titles

The Tomato Tornado

Dozens of Doughnuts

The Mysterious Meatball

Weather Report
Language Arts

Show students some examples of actual weather forecasts from newspapers or play some tape recordings of some forecasts given on the TV evening news. Have students write a weather report of their favorite foods, following the pattern in the book.

"Dinner one night consisted of lamb chops, becoming heavy at times with occasional ketchup. Periods of peas and baked potatoes were followed by gradual clearing, with a wonderful Jell-O setting in the west."

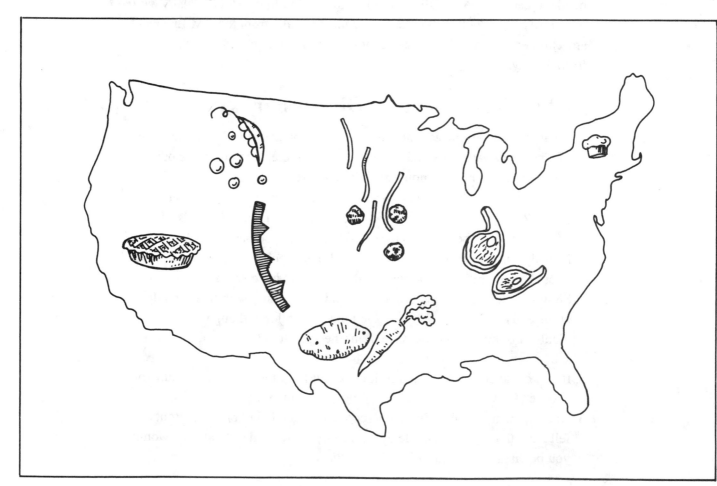

Good Enough to Eat
Art

At the end of the story, the children thought a snow-covered mountain with the sun rising behind it looked like a giant mound of mashed potatoes with a pat of butter on top. Give each child a sheet of drawing paper. Invite them to draw a picture of something in nature and then tell what food it reminds them of.

Pancakes Plus
Math

One day there was a storm of pancakes and a downpour of maple syrup in Chewandswallow. Give each student a copy of the "Pancakes Plus" reproducible on page 65. Invite each student to plan a breakfast for a specified number of guests (2, 8, 16, or 32). Students will need to rewrite the recipe to serve the appropriate number of guests and make a list of four other breakfast items they would like to serve with the pancakes. This activity can be done in pairs or small groups.

Food Groups

Health and Art

Write headings of the four food groups on the chalkboard (bread/ cereal, meat, fruit/vegetable, milk). Ask the children to name foods mentioned in the story and to write each food under the proper food group heading on the board. Give each child a copy of the "Sky Food" reproducible on page 66. Have children color each food picture and cut it out. Then each child folds a sheet of 9" x 12" construction paper into fourths and writes one food group heading in each section. Children can glue the food pictures in the correct sections of the construction paper.

Pancakes Plus

Change the pancake recipe so that it will serve the correct number of guests at your breakfast.

Pancakes for 4

Pancakes for _____

1 cup flour

1 egg

$^3/_4$ c. milk

1 T. sugar

2 T. vegetable oil

3 tsp. baking powder

$^1/_2$ tsp. salt

_____

_____

_____

_____

_____

_____

_____

Make a list of four other breakfast items you plan to serve with the pancakes.

_____

_____

_____

_____

Clouds, Rain, Wind, and Snow © 1991 Fearon Teacher Aids

Sky Food

orange juice	hamburger bun	cheese	cream cheese
peas	egg	pancakes	frankfurter
lamb chop	tomato	broccoli	milk
bread	roll	meatballs	yogurt

Clouds, Rain, Wind, and Snow © 1991 Fearon Teacher Aids

White Snow Bright Snow

Written by Alvin Tresselt and illustrated by Roger Duvoisin
New York: Lothrop, Lee & Shepard, 1947

Synopsis

Everyone senses the coming of winter. The first snowflakes fall softly from the sky until the brown earth turns white. The children enjoy catching snowflakes on their tongues, building a snow fort, and having a snowball fight. When the snowman begins to melt and the first robin appears on a bare tree branch, the children know spring has come.

Introduction

Ask the children if they have ever seen the brown earth turn white or tried to catch a lacy snowflake on their tongues. Ask the children if they have ever built a snow fort. The children in this story have. Encourage the children to listen carefully as the story is read aloud to find out what else the children see and do in *White Snow Bright Snow*.

Critical-Thinking and Discussion Questions

1. The postman, farmer, policeman, and the policeman's wife each had his or her own way of knowing it was about to snow. What are some signs that warn you when it is about to snow or rain?
2. When it actually began to snow, everyone had to prepare for the cold weather. How do you prepare for cold weather? How do you dress differently? Are there some things you cannot do in cold weather that you can do in warmer weather? What?
3. What were some of the activities the children enjoyed doing in the snow? Have you ever played in the snow? What did you do? What would you like to do in the snow that you have never done?
4. What season of the year was it when the story began? How do you know? What season was it when the snow began to fall? What season was it when the story ended? Which season was never mentioned in the story? Which is your favorite season? Why?
5. Compare the way you think the adults felt about the snow to the way you think the children felt about the snow.

Creative Writing Starters
Language Arts

I can tell that spring is near when I see _____.
If I could play in the snow, I would _____.
Snowflakes fall to the ground like _____.

Story Titles
Signs of Spring
The Secret Snow Fort
Frosty Fun

The Blizzard Edition
Language Arts

Divide the class into groups of three students each. Give each group a copy of the "Blizzard Edition" reproducible on page 71. Have each group complete the section of the daily newspaper by providing stories, interviews, and captioned pictures about the snowstorm. Or, hold mock interviews as an activity for the whole class. Ask for a student volunteer to be the reporter and several other students to be the postman, policeman, policeman's wife, farmer, or children from the story. The interviewer can ask them questions about how the snowstorm affected their lives.

Snowflakes Falling
Music and Language Arts

Ask children how they would describe snow. Point out some of the descriptive words the author used in *White Snow Bright Snow*.

> ". . . soft powdery snowflakes, whispering quietly as they sifted down."
>
> ". . . lacy snowflakes on their tongues."
>
> ". . . icy cold snowflakes sparkled in the light of the street lamps."
>
> ". . . windows peeking out from under great white eyebrows."
>
> "It filled the cold tree branches with great white blossoms."

Sing "Sh-Sh, Snowflakes Falling" by Charlotte G. Garman (*Mockingbird Flight,* Economy, 1982) with the children. This is an excellent song to help portray the silent softness of snow as it floats to the ground. Encourage children to pretend they are falling snowflakes.

Award-Winning Art
Art

White Snow Bright Snow won the Caldecott Award in 1948. The Caldecott Award honors the illustrator of a children's picture book. Flip through the book again so that children can more closely study Roger Duvoisin's work. Encourage children to notice the medium and colors the illustrator used. Provide children with black, white, gray, yellow, and red paper, paint, and crayons. Encourage children to recreate a scene from the story, using the illustrator's style. Provide paintbrushes, sponges, and cotton swabs to use with the paint. Invite children to be creative.

Snowball Count

Math

The children in the story made a snowman, a snow fort, and then had a snowball fight. Give each child a copy of the "Snowball Count" reproducible on page 72. Have children practice their math skills by calculating the correct number of snowballs for each word problem.

Editors: _____, _____, _____

Date: _____

Title:

by:

Title:

by:

Title:

by:

Snowball Count

Carefully read the sentences in the box and then answer the questions below.

> Ted had 10 snowballs.
> Judy had 2 more snowballs than Ted.
> Peter had half as many snowballs as Ted.
> Wendy had 7 fewer snowballs than Judy.
> Bob had 12 more snowballs than Peter.
> Melinda had twice as many snowballs as Ted.

1. How many snowballs did each person have?
   Ted _____
   Judy _____
   Peter _____
   Wendy _____
   Bob _____
   Melinda _____

2. How many snowballs did the boys have all together? _____

3. How many snowballs did the girls have all together? _____

4. Who had more snowballs, the girls or the boys? _____
   How many more? _____

5. How many snowballs did the children have all together? _____

6. A plastic bag will hold 10 snowballs. How many plastic bags would the children need to hold all of the snowballs? _____

Clouds, Rain, Wind, and Snow © 1991 Fearon Teacher Aids

The Snowy Day

Written and illustrated by Ezra Jack Keats
New York: Viking, 1962

Synopsis

Peter awakens to find everything covered with snow as far as he can see. He puts on his snowsuit and begins his snowy day adventure, which includes sliding down a snow-covered hill, making snow angels, and even trying to save a snowball in his pocket.

Introduction

Ask children if they have ever picked up something they found and put it in one of their pockets. Ask them what it was and why they put it in the pocket. The little boy in the story puts something he finds in his pocket. Encourage children to listen closely as the story is read aloud to find out what it is and what happens to it.

Critical-Thinking and Discussion Questions

1. What did Peter do in the snow? Which of those activities would you most like to do in the snow? Have you ever done any of them? What other things would you like to do in the snow?
2. Peter pretended to be a mountain-climber as he walked up a snowy hill. Have you ever pretended to be someone or something else? What?
3. Peter was hoping he could save the snow so that it would last longer. He was sad when he realized that the snowball he had put in his pocket had melted. Have you ever wished that you could save something so that it would last forever? What? Can you think of a time when you were having so much fun you hoped it would never end?
4. While Peter was in the bathtub that evening, he enjoyed thinking about the fun time he had in the snow. What have you done that you enjoy remembering and thinking about?
5. What do you think Peter and his friend did the next day in the deep, deep snow? Do you think Peter tried to save a snowball again? What advice would you give to Peter to help him keep a snowball from melting?

Creative Writing Starters
Language Arts

One morning when I woke up, I saw _____ .
If I could play in the snow, I would _____ .
I like to think about the time I _____ .

Story Titles
The Smiling Snowman
Secret in the Snow
Pocket Treasures

Help! I'm Melting
Language Arts

Remind students how Peter tried to save a snowball by putting it in his pocket. Ask students to pretend they were that snowball and ask the following discussion questions:

> If you had been the snowball, what would you have advised Peter to do to keep you from melting?
>
> How were you feeling inside that pocket?
>
> What do you think about when you notice that the temperature around you is getting warmer?
>
> Where is your favorite place to be?
>
> How did you feel when Peter reached in the pocket and you had melted?

Give each student a sheet of lined paper and invite them to write a paragraph about the pocket adventure from the snowball's point of view.

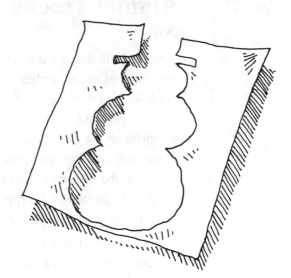

Snow Scene
Art

Give each child a 9" x 12" sheet of white construction paper and a 9" x 12" sheet of blue construction paper. Invite children to make a snow scene showing some activities they would like to do in the snow. Instruct children to tear the white sheet of paper from one corner to its diagonal corner to make a snow-covered hill. Students glue the hill to the blue sheet of construction paper. Encourage students to use the remaining white paper to tear other snow shapes to glue to their pictures. Invite children to use crayons or markers to draw themselves in the pictures and to add other details.

Snow Melt
Science

Peter tried to save a snowball in his pocket, but soon discovered it had melted. Give each child a copy of the "Snow Melt" reproducible on page 77, a cupful of snow or ice cubes, an empty cup, and a teaspoon. Have children record the starting time for their experiment on the "Snow Melt" chart. Encourage children to predict how long it will take for the snow or ice to melt completely and how many teaspoons of water will be left. Encourage children to keep a careful eye on their cups over the next few hours. When the snow or ice has completely melted, children record the ending time of the experiment. Have each child calculate and record how long it took for the snow or ice to melt. Have children transfer spoonfuls of water to the empty cup and then record the total number of teaspoons of water in the cup on the chart. Encourage students to compare and find the difference between their experiment predictions and the actual results. As an alternate experiment, give each student a cupful of snow and a cupful of ice. Have students predict which will melt the fastest and produce the most water.

Animal Tracks

Science

Peter had fun making tracks in the snow. Ask a student volunteer to trace around his or her bare foot on a sheet of construction paper and cut it out. Hold up the footprint and ask children who or what they might expect to find if they saw this print in the snow. Draw a bear pawprint on the chalkboard and ask the students who or what they might find nearby if they saw this print in the snow. Give each child a copy of the "Animal Tracks" reproducible on page 78. Ask children to guess which prints were made by which animals. Explain some features of each animal print.

Bear print—five toe prints and five claw prints above a pad

Rabbit print—two raindrop-shaped prints side by side made by the hind feet and two raindrop shapes one in front of the other made by the front feet.

Fox print—five toes on each front foot but the first toe (*dewclaw*) does not reach the ground, so the print shows only four toes. The fox only has four toes on his hind feet. When the fox walks, his hind paws step into the tracks of the front paws.

Deer print—two center toes, each protected by a strong curved hoof, which makes a crescent shape in the snow. Each crescent shape has a small dot behind that is made from the *dewclaws*, which are higher on the deer's leg.

Have children cut the worksheet on the dotted line and then cut the animal tracks apart. Invite children to glue each animal track next to the animal they think would leave that print in the snow.

Name _____

Snow Melt

Place a cup of snow or ice on your desk.

Experiment starting time _____   Experiment ending time _____

PREDICTIONS

How long do you think it will take for the snow or ice to melt? _____
How many teaspoons of water do you think will be in the cup after the
snow or ice has melted? _____

RESULTS

How long did it take the snow or ice to melt? _____
How many teaspoons of water are in the cup? _____

What is the difference between your prediction of how long it would take
the snow or ice to melt and the actual results? _____

What is the difference between your prediction of how many teaspoons
of water would be in the cup and the actual results? _____

Animal Tracks

Cut the worksheet apart on the dotted line. Cut the animal tracks apart. Glue each set of animal tracks next to the animal who would leave that print in the snow.

Grizzly Bear

Rabbit

Deer

Fox

Sparrow

Clouds, Rain, Wind, and Snow © 1991 Fearon Teacher Aids

The Snowy Day

The Snowman

Written and illustrated by Raymond Briggs
New York: Random House, 1978

Synopsis

This is a wordless book about a boy and the snowman he creates. The snowman comes to life and is fascinated by all the things the boy shows him as they tour the boy's house together. While everyone else is sleeping, the boy and the snowman share many new experiences. But having a snowman for a friend has one disadvantage—he does not last forever.

Introduction

Ask the children if they have ever built a snowman. Have children imagine what it would be like if the snowman came to life and what they would do together. Encourage children to carefully look at the pictures in this wordless book to find out what the little boy does with his new snowman friend. Be sure children are able to clearly see the pictures as you turn the pages in the book. This is best done in a small group.

Critical-Thinking and Discussion Questions

1. What did the boy use besides snow to build his snowman? If you were building a snowman, what would you use to make the eyes, nose, and mouth?
2. The boy and the snowman got in the car and pretended to drive. What do you think might have happened if they had really driven somewhere? Where do you think they would have gone? Why? If you could drive, where would you go? Why?
3. The snowman and the boy shared a meal together. If you had a friend over, what would you serve your friend for dinner?
4. The snowman was just a toy that the boy made from snow, but it came alive. Which of your toys would you like to come alive? What would you do with it?
5. The boy and the snowman flew in the sky together. Imagine what it would feel like to fly. How would your life be different if you could fly anytime and anywhere you wanted?

Creative Writing Starters
Language Arts

I would like to build a snowman because _____ .
The best way to keep a snowman from melting is to _____.
If I had a live snowman, I would take him to _____ .

Story Titles
My Snowman Is Alive!
The Big Melt
My Midnight Adventure

Snowman Chat
Language Arts

Remind the children how the author did not use any words in his story about the snowman. However, the illustrations made the unspoken dialogue between the boy and snowman quite clear. Show some of the pictures in the story and ask children to supply the dialogue. Give each child a copy of the "Snowman Chat" reproducible on page 82. Explain that the dialogue bubbles provide space for children to write a conversation between a snowman and themselves. After children have written the dialogue, invite them to illustrate the conversation.

Snowball Stack
Math

This mind-bending exercise will encourage students to use their skills of logic and reasoning. Give each child a copy of the "Snowball Stack" reproducible on page 83 and have children cut out all four snowballs. Have children set the largest snowball aside. (It can be used later to make the exercise more challenging.) Ask children to pretend that they have three pegs in a horizontal row on their desk. Ask the children to stack all three snowballs on the imaginary peg that is on their left. The snowballs must be stacked with the largest on the bottom and the smallest on top. The object of the exercise is to move all three snowballs and stack them (largest on bottom and smallest on top) on the imaginary peg on the right. This can be accomplished only by keeping the following rules in mind:

1. You can move only one snowball at a time.
2. A larger snowball can never be stacked on a smaller snow ball.

After children have experienced success, challenge them to add the fourth snowball and try the exercise again. The rules are the same, and three imaginary pegs are still used. Good Luck!

Marshmallow Snowman
Art

The little boy in the story made a snowman that came to life, but because he was made of snow, he did not last forever. Children can enjoy making this marshmallow snowman that can be their friend forever. Reproduce the "Marshmallow Snowman" reproducible on page 84 on various colors of construction paper. Give each child a copy of the reproducible and the following list of materials:

> 2 large marshmallows (for body)
> $1/2$ of a large marshmallow (cut horizontally for hat)
> 4 miniature marshmallows
> scissors

Have children cut out the pieces on the reproducible and assemble the snowman according to the picture. Invite children to add facial features, using Q-tips and food coloring.

The Big Melt
Science

The little boy's snowman melted at the end of the story. Explain to children that the melting point is the temperature at which a substance changes from a solid to a liquid. The melting point of different substances varies. Explore the conditions necessary to cause various substances to melt and the state that they are changed into by conducting the following experiments:

1. Put a slice of cheese on a piece of bread and place it in a toaster oven.
2. Put some crayon shavings between two pieces of waxed paper and run a warm iron over them.
3. Place a chocolate bar in the warm sun for a few hours.

Invite children to describe and compare the state of each substance before and after it melted, predict how much heat or how long it will take for each substance to melt, and evaluate the results of the experiments.

Snowman Chat

Write a conversation between yourself and a snowman.
Illustrate your conversation.

Clouds, Rain, Wind, and Snow © 1991 Fearon Teacher Aids

Name _____

Snowball Stack

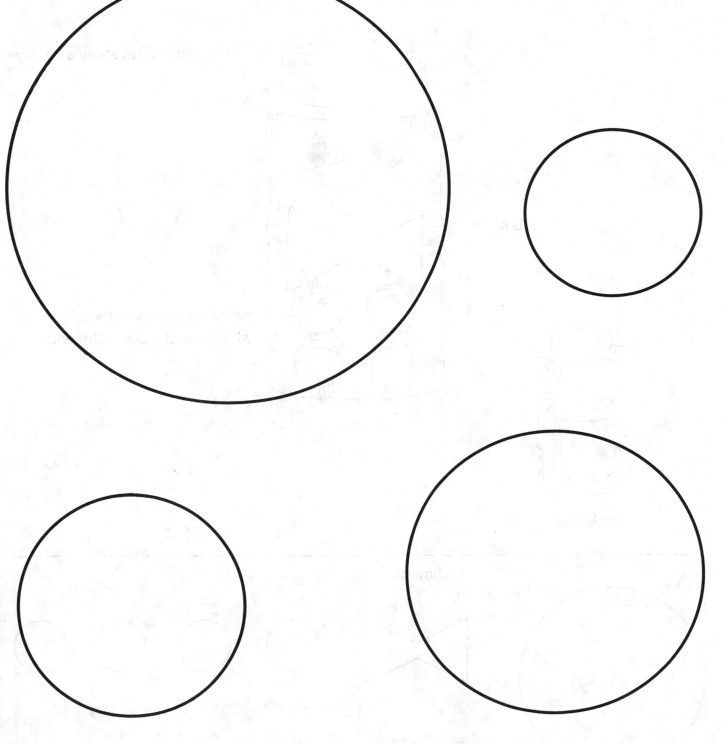

The Snowman

Marshmallow Snowman

Carefully cut out the pieces below the dotted line. Assemble your snowman.

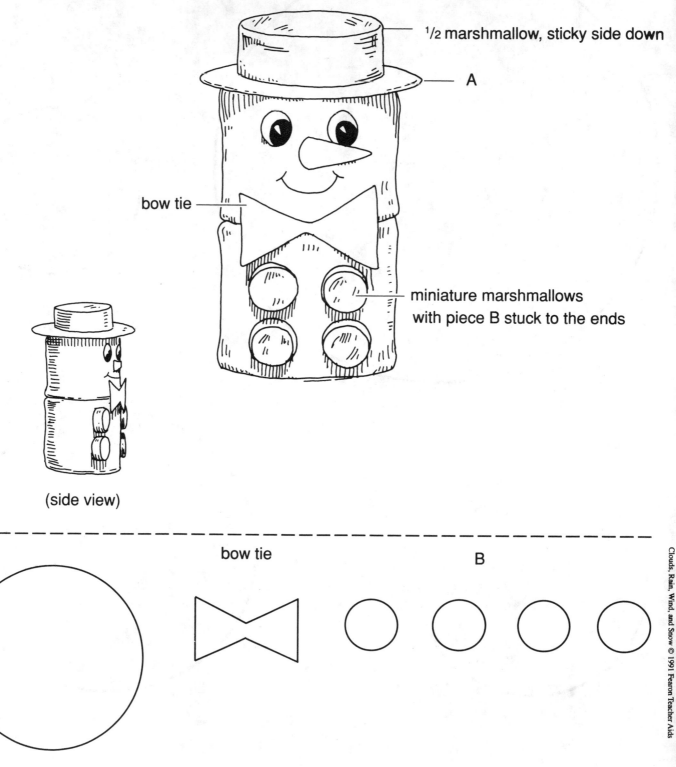

½ marshmallow, sticky side down

A

bow tie

miniature marshmallows
with piece B stuck to the ends

(side view)

- -

A

bow tie

B

Clouds, Rain, Wind, and Snow © 1991 Fearon Teacher Aids

The Snowman

Katy and the Big Snow

Written and illustrated by Virginia Lee Burton
Boston: Houghton Mifflin, 1943

Synopsis

Katy, the crawler tractor, is given the important job of plowing through some very deep snow to rescue the city of Geoppolis. Katy proves her dependability and determination by not quitting until the task is complete.

Introduction

Ask children if they have ever been given something to do that seemed too difficult, and if so, how they handled the situation. Ask children if they have ever been unable to finish a job because they were too tired. In this story, Katy is given a big job that makes her very tired. Encourage the children to listen closely as the story is read aloud to find out if Katy is able to complete the job.

Critical-Thinking and Discussion Questions

1. The truck plows did the snow plowing when the snow was lighter. Katy, the crawler tractor, was always given the job of snow plowing when the snow was very heavy. Would you rather be a truck plow and have an easy job or a crawler tractor and have a more difficult job? Why?

2. When Katy pulled the steamroller out of the pond, the Highway Department was very proud of her. Have you ever done something that made someone else very proud of you? Have you ever been very proud of yourself for completing some tough job? What?

3. Katy had the determination to finish her job even when she began to feel tired. What do you think would have happened to the city of Geoppolis if Katy had said that she was simply too tired to finish?

4. The people of Geoppolis knew they could depend on Katy. Why do you think they knew she could do the job? Do other people consider you to be dependable?

5. Do you think Katy was a hero? Why? What do you think it means to be a hero? Who do you consider to be a hero?

Creative Writing Starters

Language Arts

The hardest job I ever had to do was _____.

When I get tired I usually _____ .

I like to help out by _____ .

Story Titles

The Big Snow

My Toughest Job

Don't Quit Now

Katy's Diary

Language Arts

Encourage children to think about how Katy felt throughout the story. Ask children how Katy might have felt about working on the roads in the summer, how she felt about having to stay at home when there was not enough snow for her to plow, or how she felt when she had successfully plowed the snow throughout the whole city of Geoppolis. Give each child a copy of the "Katy's Diary" reproducible on page 89. Using the first person, invite children to write down some of the events that took place in the story from Katy's point of view.

Telephone for Help
Language Arts

Remind children about how the Chief of Police called Katy for help. Use this opportunity to review the correct procedure students should use to call for help in emergency situations. Review what information should be given, including the location and type of emergency. Encourage children to work in pairs to practice making and receiving emergency phone calls. Invite pairs of children to present their phone calls for the class. Tape record the calls and play them back. Discuss clarity and response.

City of Geoppolis
Social Studies

Show children the large yellow map of Geoppolis near the beginning of the book. Point out that each numbered red flag stands for some specific place in Geoppolis. The small pictures around the border of the map explain what each number on the map represents. Give each child a copy of the "Map of a City" reproducible on page 90. Invite children to color the map and to become familiar with the location of each of the seven places. After children finish coloring, ask them to place a finger on the flag that stands for the hospital. Ask them to use their fingers to "walk" to the Water Department. Ask them to tell you which direction they traveled. Ask other questions to give the children map-reading practice.

> If you start at the Post Office and travel west, what building will you come to?
>
> Put your finger on the Police Department. Walk to the Chicken Farm. Which direction did you travel?
>
> If you begin at the Chicken Farm and walk east, will you arrive at the Library or the Water Department?

Snowflake Mural
Art

Divide children into groups of three or four students. Give each group a large piece of colored butcher paper and several 6" squares of lightweight white paper to make a snowflake mural. Invite children to fold the 6" squares in half each direction and then into a triangular shape. Children can cut out V shapes, half circles, or any other design on each of the three sides of the triangle. When the paper is unfolded, it will be a beautiful and unique snowflake. After all the snowflakes are cut out, encourage children to work together to arrange and glue them in a pleasing pattern on the colored butcher paper. Have each group hold their finished mural up so that the class can see it. Encourage each group member to point out the part he or she had in making the mural.

Katy's Diary

Pretend that you are Katy, the crawler tractor. Write down some of the things that happened to you in the story and how you felt about them.

_____

_____

_____

_____

_____

_____

_____

_____

_____

_____

_____

_____

_____

_____

_____

_____

_____

Map of a City

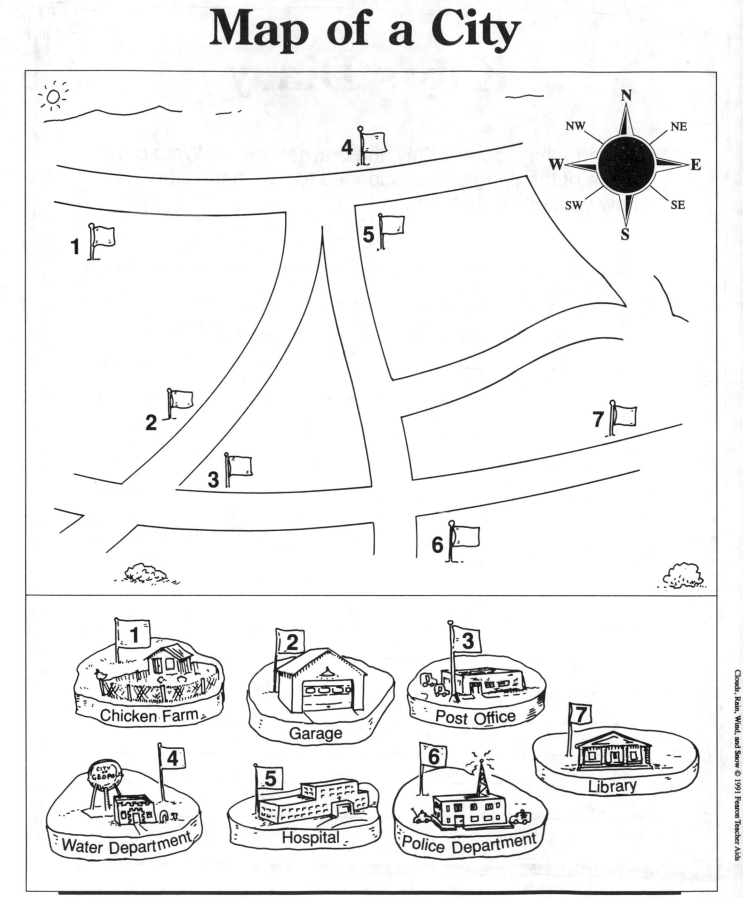

The Big Snow

Written and illustrated by Berta and Elmer Hader
New York: Macmillan, 1948

Synopsis

The animals of the woods and meadow know that when the geese fly south, it is a sign the countryside will soon be covered by a deep blanket of snow. All the animals, big and small, begin to gather food and search for a warm, snug place to spend the cold winter. If not for the help of a generous little old man and woman, many of the animals would have experienced some hungry days while waiting for the warm spring to come.

Introduction

"Always be prepared" is a motto that many people believe is important to think about. Ask children what they think it means to be prepared. The animals in the story knew that they needed to prepare for the cold winter. Encourage children to listen closely as the story is read aloud to find out what the animals do to prepare and why.

Critical-Thinking and Discussion Questions

1. When the animals saw the geese flying overhead, they knew it was time to prepare for the Big Snow. They had to think ahead and plan for the future. Have you ever prepared for something you knew was going to happen? What did you do? Did your preparations pay off? How? Have you ever been unprepared? How did you feel?

2. Why did the animals have trouble finding food after the snow fell?

3. What do you think might have happened to the animals if the little old man and woman had not scattered seeds, nuts, and bread crumbs on the ground?

4. Do you think the little old man and woman will scatter food for the animals next winter? Do you think the animals will remember that and count on the little old man and woman as a source of food?

5. The deer and squirrel understood that the crow's caw meant there was food. How do you think the animals knew that? Do you think animals can communicate with one another? Do you think they understand and help each other? How do you know?

6. Some of the animals in the story hibernated during the winter, some of them went south to a warmer climate, and some of them stayed active during the cold weather. If you were an animal, which would you rather do? Why?

Creative Writing Starters
Language Arts

I think the little old man and woman were _____ .
If I were an animal preparing for the winter, I would _____ .
The animal I would least like to be during the winter is a _____
    because _____ .

Story Titles
Caught Unprepared
The Crow's Caw
Food, Food, Food

Animal Concentration
Language Arts

Divide children into several student pairs. Reproduce the animal and name cards on page 96 on construction paper and give each pair of children a copy. Have the children cut the cards apart and spread them out on a table or the floor, face down. Each child takes a turn at this game of concentration by turning two cards over to match an animal picture with the animal's name. If the cards match, they are removed. If a match is not made, the cards are turned back over. Children continue taking turns until all cards have been matched.

Guess My Word

Language Arts

Write the words listed below from the story on 3" x 5" cards and give one card to each student. Have children write clues from the story or a definition to describe the word. Collect all the cards and then divide the class into two teams. Begin with one player from each team and read the definition or clue from one of the cards. The first player to say the correct word being described earns a point for his or her team. Continue until all the cards have been read and each team member has had a turn to guess.

caw	snow	sleep
winter	moon	cold
nibble	branches	carrot
geese	sniff	coat
south	spring	squirrel
seed	shelter	hillside
food	hunt	trail
underground	hungry	clouds
deer	scatter	roof
fly		

To continue the word study, put the words into two categories as a class—verbs and nouns.

Invite a Bird to Dinner

Science

Remind children of the various types of birds mentioned in the story and how the little old man and woman scattered seeds and bread crumbs on the ground for the birds to enjoy. Divide the class into groups of four or five students and give each group an egg carton to make a bird feeder. Have each group cut off the top of the egg carton and use a small nail to punch a drainage hole in the bottom of each egg "cup." The children fill two cups with sand or gravel. This will not only help keep the light-weight carton from blowing away but will also provide grit for the birds. Have children fill the rest of the cups with wild bird seed, sun-flower seeds, bread crumbs, or cracked corn. Place the feeders outside. If you live in a windy area, anchor the carton by nailing it to a piece of lumber or by driving a nail through it into the ground. Watch your dinner guests enjoy the feast! (Read *Invite a Bird to Dinner* by Beverly Courtney Crook, 1978.)

Be Prepared

Art and Science

Discuss how the various animals and birds in *The Big Snow* prepared for the cold winter. Then give each child a 9" x 12" sheet of construction paper to make a "Be Prepared" poster. Have children write "Be Prepared" in large letters across the top of the poster. Invite children to choose an animal or bird mentioned in the book and draw a picture of it preparing for the Big Snow. At the bottom of the picture, have students write one sentence that describes the preparations the animal or bird is making. Display the posters around the classroom or combine them together to make a class booklet.

raccoon	squirrel	skunk	rabbit
deer	blue jay	owl	mouse

The Big Snow